Paige Scarbrough

DATE DUE		
NOV		
JA		
601A		
JAN 2 3		

5836   9.00

523.1   Darling, David J.
Dar

              **Galaxies : cities of
              stars.**

THE GALAXIES

THE GALAXIES
CITIES OF STARS

by David J. Darling

Illustrated by Jeanette Swofford

DILLON PRESS, INC.   MINNEAPOLIS, MINNESOTA

Photographs are reproduced through the courtesy of the California Institute of Technology, the Cerro Tololo Inter-American Observatory, Hale Observatories, the Kitt Peak National Observatory, and the National Radio Astronomy Observatory, operated by Associated Universities, Inc. under contract with the National Science Foundation (NRAO observers: Ronald D. Ekers; Ulrich J. Schwarz; W. Miller Goss; Alan H. Bridle; Richard A. Perley).

Dillon Press, Inc., 242 Portland Avenue South
Minneapolis, Minnesota 55415

Printed in the United States of America

Library of Congress Cataloging in Publication Data

Darling, David J.
    Galaxies : cities of stars.

    Bibliography: p.
    Includes index.
    Summary: Explains what galaxies are, how they were formed, and the types of galaxies.
    1. Galaxies—Juvenile literature [1. Galaxies]
I. Title.
QB857.3.D37   1985   523.1′12   84-23092
ISBN 0-87518-285-2

3   4   5   6   7   8   9   10   91   90   89   88   87

Contents

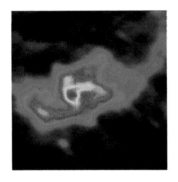

Galaxy Facts

Our Own: the Milky Way, an ordinary spiral galaxy which contains more than 100 billion stars and is at least 400,000 light-years across

Spiral: about one-third of all galaxies in space are spiral-shaped star cities like our own Milky Way

Elliptical: more than half of all galaxies are called ellipticals, some round while others are more oval, or stretched out, in shape

Irregular: about one in every ten galaxies is called irregular, which means that it has no definite shape

Largest: the giant radio galaxy 3C-236, which measures 18 million light-years from end to end

Smallest: the dwarf irregular galaxy GR-8, which is just 1,000 light-years across

Closest: two irregular galaxies, the large and small Magellanic clouds, are satellites of the Milky Way and our closest galactic neighbors. They are less than 200,000 light-years away

Farthest: some quasars are more than 10 billion light-years away. Scientists believe that quasars may be the very bright nuclei of young galaxies

Questions & Answers About Galaxies

Q. How do we know what kind of galaxy we live in if we can't see it from the outside?
A. Radio waves of a very special type have allowed scientists to find out where much of the cold hydrogen gas in our galaxy is located. The gas is concentrated into great, winding arms, showing that ours is a spiral galaxy.

Q. Why do radio waves and infrared rays reach us from the center of the Galaxy, but not ordinary light?
A. Light coming from the center is blocked by thick clouds of dust in the Galaxy's disk. Radio, infrared, and some other types of radiation are not affected by the dust and so pass right through.

Q. What are spiral arms?
A. Parts of a spiral galaxy's disk where most of the dust, gas, and large, bright stars are found.

Q. What are the largest and the smallest galaxies known?
A. The giant radio galaxy 3C-236 measures 18 million light-years from end to end. By contrast, the dwarf irregular galaxy GR-8 has a diameter of only 1,000 light-years.

Q. Can galaxies explode?
A. Scientists are not sure. Some galaxies look as though they are exploding. On the other hand, it is possible that in these galaxies there is a sudden burst of star formation taking place.

Q. Do galaxies ever crash into each other?
A. Yes, occasionally. When this happens, the two galaxies pull each other out of shape or become mixed up together. Unusual "ring galaxies" may also be formed during these giant collisions.

Q. Is there anything in the space between galaxies?
A. Scientists have found that all clusters of galaxies give off X rays. Recently, this has been shown to be due to very hot, thin gas spread over much of intergalactic space.

Q. How far are we from the middle of our Local Supercluster?
A. About 65 million light years. Close to the center itself is the giant elliptical galaxy NGC 4486, in the Virgo cluster.

Q. What is the most distant quasar known?
A. PKS 2000-330. It is thought to be about 13 billion light-years away.

WIDE-ANGLE VIEW OF THE MILKY WAY FROM EARTH IN THE DIRECTION OF ITS CENTER

1 What Are Galaxies?

Imagine that we are astronauts of the future floating somewhere in space. Ahead of us is a huge, bright object that looks like a giant pinwheel. Its long, glowing arms spiral out from a bright center. Coming closer to the great object, we start to see sparkling points of light dotted along the spiral arms. They are stars! Still closer, we see more points of light, and then more and more. The pinwheel, it turns out, is a **galaxy***—a huge city of stars.

Now we're at the edge of the Galaxy and can guess its size. Containing more than 100 **billion** stars, it is hundreds of thousands of **trillions** of miles across. It is so big that light, traveling at 186,000 miles per second, takes more than 400,000 years to cross from one side of it to the other.

Stars begin to fly past us as we plunge into one of the gleaming spiral arms. We can tell that we're in the outer parts of the Galaxy, well away from the busy center. But where are we heading?

Suddenly, an ordinary yellow star appears in front of us and grows brighter and brighter as we approach. Soon we realize that it's the sun—the star around which the earth moves. We have flown into our own galaxy from far out in space, and arrived home again!

*Words in **bold type** are explained in the glossary at the end of this book.

The Milky Way

Gazing into the sky from earth on a clear, dark night, we can see what our galaxy looks like from the inside. First, we see about 2,000 separate stars scattered over the sky in all directions. These are the brightest stars because they are all fairly close to us in space.

Next, as our eyes get used to the dark, we notice a hazy, glowing band that stretches across the sky from north to south. This is the **Milky Way.** Through binoculars or a telescope, we find that it, too, is starry. In fact, the Milky Way is made up of **millions** upon millions of distant stars! The thin band of the Milky Way contains most of the distant stars in the Galaxy that can be seen from earth. To find out why, let's look at the whole Galaxy in a different way.

This close-up photo of the Andromeda Galaxy—a spiral galaxy like our own—shows how the Milky Way Galaxy may look from the outside. Its bulging middle is surrounded by a pancake-shaped disk.

As we discovered during our imaginary space trip, the Galaxy, seen from above, is spiral in shape. Seen from the side, though, it would look more like two giant cymbals that had been crashed together. It has a bright, bulging middle, which is surrounded by a broader, pancake-shaped **disk.**

Looking out from earth away from the Galaxy's disk, we see only a few stars. But looking in a direction along the disk—through the thickest part of the Galaxy—we see a huge star swarm. It is this swarm that appears in our sky as the Milky Way.

Actually, there are many parts of the Galaxy that we can't see from earth. But because the Milky Way is the biggest part that we can see, scientists named the whole of our star city—the **Milky Way Galaxy**—after it.

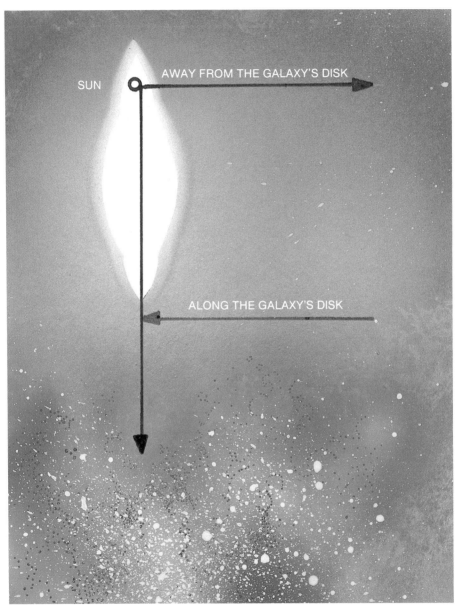

SUN

AWAY FROM THE GALAXY'S DISK

ALONG THE GALAXY'S DISK

In this drawing the Milky Way Galaxy is seen from the side from a point outside the Galaxy. The arrow pointing down from the sun shows the direction of the Milky Way, along the galaxy's disk, from earth. The arrow pointing to the right shows a view from earth away from the disk in which many fewer stars are visible.

Galaxies of All Kinds

In one year, light travels about 6 trillion miles (9½ trillion kilometers), a distance called one **light-year.** The Galaxy in which we live is over 400,000 light-years across. Yet, even this is a tiny distance in the vastness of space.

Through large telescopes, we can see many other galaxies—each a star city like our own—scattered about the universe. Most are millions of light-years away. In all of space, scientists think there may be as many as a billion galaxies. The ones farthest away from us gave off the light we are now receiving from them more than 5 billion years ago, before even the sun was born!

No two galaxies are exactly alike. Yet, in their studies of space objects, astronomers have found that there are just a few main types.

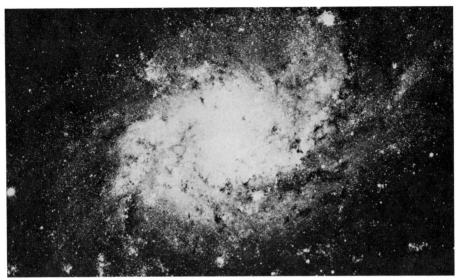

This photo, taken at the Kitt Peak National Observatory, shows a spiral galaxy in the constellation of Triangulum. The spiral arms and pinwheel shape of a spiral galaxy are plainly visible.

First, there are **spiral galaxies.** Seen from above, these have beautiful spiral arms and pinwheel shapes.

Then, there are **elliptical galaxies.** These differ in shape from perfectly round balls to squashed ovals and are the most common of star cities.

Finally, there are **irregular galaxies.** These are collections of stars with no definite shape at all.

Galaxies differ greatly in size. At one extreme, there are **dwarfs** barely 1,000 light-years across that have about 100,000 stars. At the other, there are **giants** several hundred thousand to millions of light-years across that contain as many as a trillion stars.

We happen to live in an ordinary spiral galaxy. And it is here, within the Milky Way, that we begin our **galactic** journey.

16

The fuzzy, oval-shaped object at the center of this photo is an elliptical galaxy. It is located in the constellation of Virgo.

An irregular galaxy in the constellation of Ursa Major is shown above. The galaxy does not have a defined spiral, oval, or round shape.

SIDE VIEW OF THE GALAXY

SUN'S POSITION
IN GALAXY

NUCLEUS

DISK

TOP VIEW OF
THE GALAXY

TWO VIEWS OF THE MILKY WAY GALAXY

2 The Galaxy Around Us

The view we have of the Milky Way Galaxy is a very special one—from the *inside*. Along with the sun and the other planets, we live in the "suburbs" of our great star city, 30,000 light-years from the center. In fact, we are inside a spiral arm roughly halfway out towards the rim of the Galaxy's disk.

We move, with the rest of the Galaxy, about its center. But it takes us a very long time to go around one full turn. Even traveling at 137 miles per second (220 kilometers per second), the trips lasts 230 million years!

Our position inside the Milky Way makes studies of the Galaxy difficult. It's almost like trying to draw a picture of the outside of a house having spent our whole lives within one of its rooms. Yet, gradually, we're beginning to uncover the mysteries of the Galaxy and to learn some of its innermost secrets.

Astronomers have found that the star city around us has four main parts. Let's now look at each of these parts in turn.

Disk and Nucleus

First is the wide, flattened disk that we have already described. Measuring at least 120,000 light-years across,

This photo of a spiral galaxy in the constellation of Pisces shows how the Milky Way Galaxy may look from above.

and about 1,500 light-years in depth, it is where the spiral arms of the Galaxy lie.

The disk, and especially the spiral arms, contain what scientists call **Population I** objects. These are objects that are young compared with the Galaxy as a whole. They include the youngest, brightest, hottest stars of all—the **O-type** and **B-type** stars—which may shine tens of thousands of times more brightly than the sun. Often, O- and B-type stars are found in groups called **galactic clusters.**

Other Population I objects, also gathered in the disk's spiral arms, include ordinary stars such as the sun and huge clouds of gas and dust. It's from these clouds that new stars will form. At the same time, the gas and dust act like a thick fog and block out our view of the disk beyond a

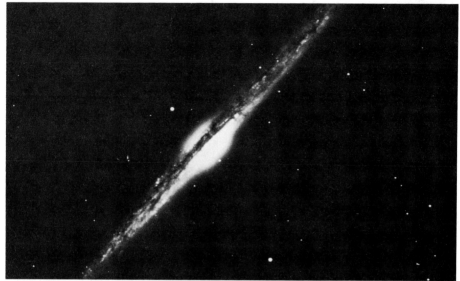

In this side view of a spiral galaxy in the constellation of Coma Berenices, its bulging middle, or nucleus, stands out from the surrounding disk.

Galactic clusters in the constellation of Cassiopeia are shown above. These O-type and B-type stars are examples of Population I objects.

The Rosette Nebula in the constellation of Monoceros contains a large number of Population I objects.

The bulging middle, or nucleus, of the great galaxy in Andromeda is shown above. Many Population II objects—mainly old, small, dim, red stars—are found in the nucleus of such galaxies.

few thousand light-years from earth.

If we could take away the gas and dust, we would have a wonderful view of the second main part of our galaxy. This is its bulging middle, or **nucleus,** measuring about 16,000 light-years across.

The nucleus is the home of **Population II** objects. These are mostly small, dim, red stars that are nearly as old as the Galaxy itself. From far out in space, the nucleus would seem to glow red while the spiral arms around it, with their brighter, hotter stars, would shine white or blue-white.

Astronomers can't see inside the nucleus by ordinary light. Still, they know that the stars there must be crowded much closer together than they are in the spiral arms. They also know, by looking at invisible rays called

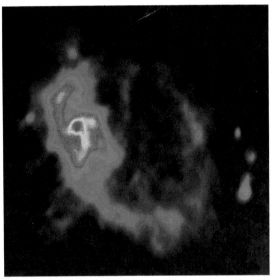

This image of the nucleus of the Milky Way Galaxy was received in the form of radio emissions by the Very Large Array (VLA) in New Mexico. The VLA is a series of twenty-seven widely spaced radio telescopes.

radio waves, infrared, and **X rays,** that something strange is happening in the **core,** the region at the center of the nucleus.

Although the core is only 1,000 light-years across, it contains as much matter as several hundred million suns. Some of this matter is in the form of giant gas clouds. The rest is crammed into a tiny space within the core just a few light-years across.

Right at the center of our galaxy there is something very small, yet very heavy. Some scientists think that it may be a **black hole**—an object whose pull of **gravity** is so strong that not even light can escape from it. Around the black hole, there may be a fantastic whirlpool of hot gas and dust. We need to learn much more about the core before we know for sure what is really there!

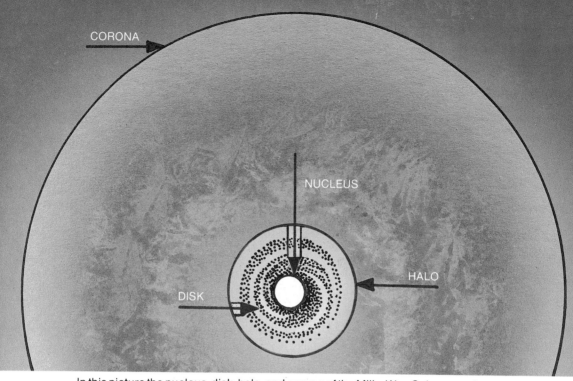

CORONA

NUCLEUS

HALO

DISK

In this picture the nucleus, disk, halo, and corona of the Milky Way Galaxy are shown. Including the halo and corona, the Galaxy is much larger than just its bright, highly visible parts—the nucleus and the disk.

Halo and Corona

Surrounding the bright nucleus and disk is the third important part of the Galaxy—the **halo.** Like the nucleus, this contains old, Population II stars. But unlike the nucleus, the halo is a round region of space 160,000 light-years across. It forms a giant bubble in which both the nucleus and the disk lie.

Many of the halo stars are scattered very thinly through space. For this reason, the halo shines only dimly. Some halo stars, though, are packed tightly into **globular clusters.** Among the 100 or so known globular clusters, the largest contains more than a million stars.

Outside the halo is an even larger bubble. This huge area is the **corona**—the fourth, and most recently discovered, part of the Milky Way Galaxy. Scientists think that it

25

Many thousands of stars are concentrated in this globular cluster in the constellation of Hercules. Star clusters like this one are found in the halo of the Milky Way Galaxy.

is at least 400,000 light-years across and about ten times as heavy as the rest of the Galaxy put together!

In spite of its weight, the corona seems to contain no bright stars. Perhaps its dark matter is in the form of stars that have died. Or, as some scientists think, the corona may be filled with a vast army of tiny, ghostlike particles called **neutrinos.**

It will be some time before we learn all the secrets of the Milky Way. Meanwhile, astronomers are working hard to solve other mysteries in the galaxies beyond our own.

GALAXY, TYPE Sc, IN THE CONSTELLATION OF CEPHEUS

3 **The Great Galactic Zoo**

We have already seen that there are three main types of galaxies: spiral, elliptical, and irregular. Now, let's look more closely at differences within, and among, each of these types.

Spiral Galaxies

About one-third of all galaxies in space are spiral-shaped star cities like our own. But, seen through a telescope, no two look exactly the same.

Scientists divide ordinary spirals into three families—*Sa, Sb,* and *Sc*—depending on how tightly the spiral arms are wrapped around the nucleus. Usually, the more spread out or "open" the arms are, the smaller the nucleus is.

Sa galaxies have the faintest, most tightly wound arms, while Sc galaxies have the brightest, most loosely wound. The Milky Way Galaxy lies somewhere between these two and is thought to be a type Sb spiral.

There are also spiral galaxies of a completely different kind that have bright bars running through their nuclei. These are the **barred spirals.** Their spiral arms sprout from the ends of their bars and, as with normal spirals, they can be divided into three groups. Depending on how

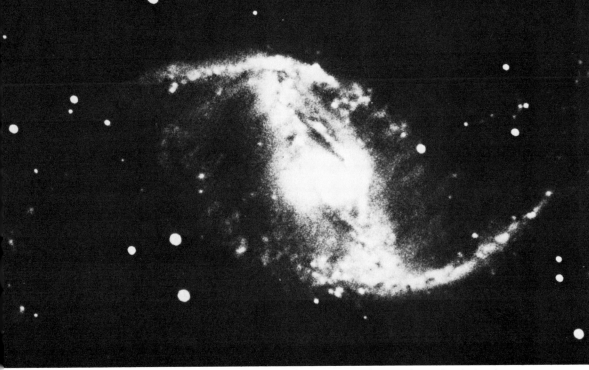

This photo, taken at Kitt Peak National Observatory, shows a barred spiral galaxy, type SBb, in the constellation of Camelopardalis. The galaxy's spiral arms extend from the end of its bars.

tightly wound their arms are, barred spirals are called *SBa*, *SBb*, or *SBc*.

In size, spiral galaxies may be anywhere from 20,000 light-years to more than 100,000 light-years across. But this distance only includes the bright disk that we can easily see. As in the case of the Milky Way, distant galaxies may be surrounded by much larger, but fainter, halos and coronas. The largest of spiral galaxies, then, may actually reach across half a million light-years in space!

An important fact about spirals, whether normal or barred, is that they contain a great deal of gas and dust. These are the raw materials from which new stars are made. In spiral galaxies they are concentrated—along with other young (Population I) objects that have recently formed from the gas and dust—in the long, winding arms

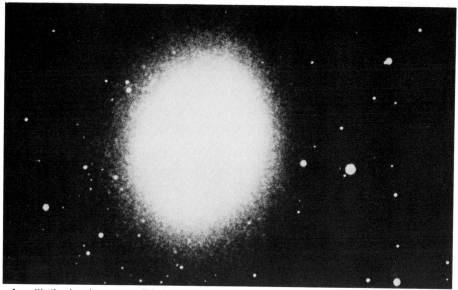

An elliptical galaxy, type E2, is shown here. Located in the constellation of Andromeda, this galaxy has a shape that is more nearly round than oval.

of the disk. One type of galaxy, though, does not have such a star factory.

Elliptical Galaxies

More than half of all galaxies are ellipticals. Some are completely round, while others are oval in shape. Elliptical galaxies are given numbers to describe how stretched out they appear. At one extreme, an *E0* elliptical is almost perfectly round. At the other, a type *E7* has a very squashed oval shape.

Elliptical galaxies come in a tremendous range of sizes. Most are dwarfs, as small as 5,000 light-years across. A few are giant ellipticals measuring hundreds of thousands of light-years across and containing up to a trillion stars.

31

This giant elliptical galaxy is found in the constellation of Virgo. Since it is almost perfectly round, it is a type E0 galaxy.

Unlike spiral galaxies, ellipticals have almost no gas and dust. As a result, they have nothing with which to build new stars.

All of the stars inside elliptical galaxies are old (Population II) objects. Some are packed within globular clusters. There may be hundreds of these clusters in the halos of the larger ellipticals. The rest of the stars form the main body of the galaxy, which is almost like a vast globular cluster itself.

Irregular Galaxies

About one in every ten galaxies has no definite shape at all. This group is called the irregular galaxies. Like spirals, they contain a lot of gas and dust from which new stars are being formed. But irregular galaxies are usually

The large Magellanic cloud is an irregular galaxy located in the constellation of Dorado.

quite small. They range between about 1,000 light-years and 25,000 light-years across.

Two irregular galaxies, the large and small **Magellanic clouds,** are our closest galactic neighbors. In fact, they are actually **satellites** of the Milky Way. As satellites they are forced to go around our galaxy, because of its pull of gravity, in the same way that the moon is forced to go around the earth.

We have looked at the three main forms that galaxies may take, and at some of the differences among them. Now let's try to answer a really difficult question: Where did galaxies come from?

The Origin of Star Cities

Scientists believe that the entire universe began to

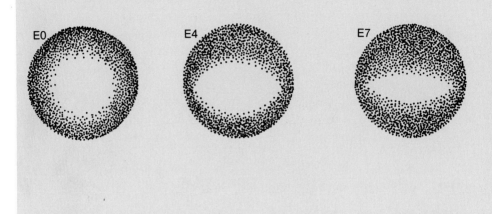

These diagrams show the shapes of various elliptical and spiral galaxies. Elliptical galaxies ranging from round to extremely oval in shape are represented on the left-

form about 15 billion years ago. Most think that it appeared as a result of a huge explosion called the Big Bang.

At first, the whole of space was filled with a hot "soup" of particles. Then, several hundred million years after the Big Bang, large clouds of hydrogen gas started to form. From these came the **protogalaxies,** or galaxies in the making.

Slowly, because of their own gravity, the protogalaxies pulled themselves together. As they became smaller, they started to turn faster.

About one billion years after the Big Bang, the first galaxies—with the first stars inside them—began to appear. Whether elliptical, spiral, or irregular, all the galaxies at this early stage had large amounts of gas and dust in them. Their first stars probably were big, bright,

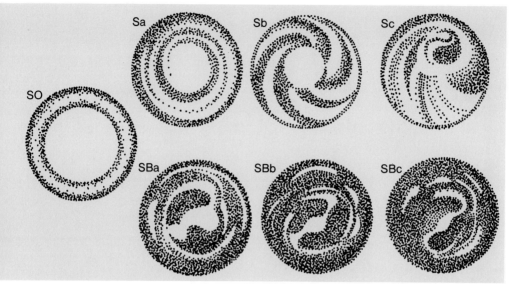

hand page. Tightly and loosely wound spiral and barred spiral galaxies are represented on the right.

bluish-white O- and B-types—stars that form especially well in gassy, dusty regions.

Scientists would like to know if the galaxies long ago really did look bluer than they do today. If they did, we would know that galaxies change as they grow older. To find out, we start with the fact that the universe is like a time machine. As we look deeper into space, we also look back into time.

Using the largest telescopes, astronomers have studied galaxies that are at least 7 billion light-years away. In other words, these star cities are being seen now as they were 7 billion years ago when the universe was only half as old as it is today!

The first results are very exciting. The distant galaxies definitely appear bluer than those of the present

QUASAR

day. But can we look back even further, to a time when the first galaxies had only just formed? To answer this question, we must come face to face with the most incredible objects yet found in the universe—the mighty **quasars.**

GALAXY

Scientists have proposed different theories to explain how galaxies were formed. In this drawing, an artist pictures a quasar on the left. Its strong pull of gravity attracts huge amounts of matter that form a galaxy.

QUASAR 3C-273 IN THE CONSTELLATION OF VIRGO

4 Quasars and Galaxies

Seen through a telescope, a quasar doesn't seem very exciting. It looks like an ordinary blue star, much like countless other blue stars scattered across the Milky Way.

But scientists have found that there is far more to quasars than meets the eye. They are not, in fact, stars in our own galaxy. Instead, they are the most distant objects yet discovered!

Some quasars are more than 10 billion light-years away. To appear as bright as they do, at such enormous distances, quasars must shine between a hundred and a thousand times more brightly than a galaxy like the Milky Way.

Quasars give off not only light, but often radio waves, infrared, X rays, and other kinds of waves as well. Strangest of all, they seem to pour out all this **energy** from a tiny region less than a light-year across!

What objects could possibly be so small, yet shine so brightly? And, why do we see them only in the universe of far away and long ago?

The Quasar Monster

There are very few ways that scientists know of in which more energy than a hundred normal galaxies can

This is an artist's view of what a black hole might look like in the center of an active galaxy. Matter from surrounding stars and other objects in space is drawn into the

come from a space less than a light-year across. One source of such concentrated power is a black hole.

Let's imagine that the "energy monster" deep inside a quasar is a very heavy black hole. It might weigh several billion times as much as the sun, yet be small enough to fit inside the area of our **solar system.**

Let's also imagine that the energy monster has a supply of "food." This could be in the form of great clouds of gas and dust in the space around it.

Because of its strong gravity, the black hole could suck this gas and dust into a fast-spinning whirlpool around itself. Just before falling into the black hole, the gas and dust would become tremendously hot. They would give off huge amounts of energy. This energy, escaping into space as light and other, invisible rays, would

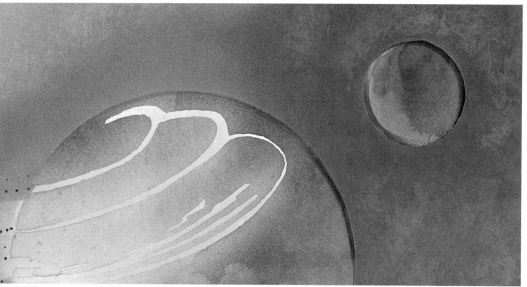

area of the black hole by its extremely powerful pull of gravity.

be enough to provide the quasar with its great brightness.

Quasars are not the only objects that may have such powerful, energy-making black holes inside them. As we have already seen, some scientists think there may be a black hole at the center of the Milky Way. What's more, we know of other star cities throughout the universe in whose cores there may lurk dark and hungry energy monsters!

From Quasar to Galaxy

Scientists have now studied some quasars very closely. In every case, they have found that what at first looked like a tiny bright point is really surrounded by a faint "fuzziness." This fuzziness is almost certainly due to a great mass of stars. Could it be, then, that quasars are the very bright nuclei of young galaxies?

It's possible that as some galaxies formed, the matter deep inside them was pushed tightly together. This squashing action could have led to the birth of the first black holes.

In the early stages of such galaxies, there would be plenty of gas and dust to feed the energy monsters. The fiery whirlpools around the black holes would be well filled with captured matter. During this time, the nuclei of the young galaxies would grow very bright. They would appear, from far off, as quasars.

Later on, as the food supply ran low, the nuclei would grow dimmer. Eventually, just ordinary galaxies would be left behind.

This is only one of the exciting ideas that scientists

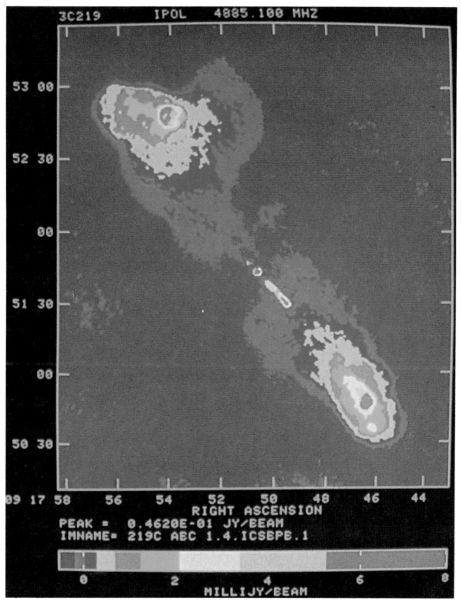

This false-color image shows the extended lobes, hot spots, and a short jet extending from the core of the radio galaxy 3C-219. The hot spots are believed to be the emissions from high-pressure regions formed at the end of jets that transport energy from the core of the galaxy to the lobes.

have proposed in which quasars and galaxies are linked. The theory explains well why we see no quasars in the universe today. It explains, too, why there are **active galaxies**—objects that appear partway between true quasars and normal galaxies like our own.

The Missing Links

Active galaxies are cities of stars that give off unusually large amounts of energy. They come in several different types.

First, there are **radio galaxies.** These look like giant ellipticals when seen through an ordinary telescope. Unlike normal galaxies, they give off huge amounts of radio waves. Often, most of their radio energy comes from regions lying far beyond the bright star cities themselves.

At the center of this photo is a Seyfert galaxy in the constellation of Perseus. The nuclei of Seyfert galaxies give off huge amounts of energy and are far brighter than those of normal spiral galaxies.

Then, there are **Seyfert galaxies.** These are spiral, rather than elliptical in shape. But they, too, give off an enormous amount of energy. Most of it comes from their nuclei, which are far brighter than those of normal spiral galaxies and look almost starlike.

Finally, there are objects with even brighter, smaller nuclei called **N-galaxies** and **BL Lacertae** objects. These seem to be the actual missing links between quasars and the normal galactic forms.

Could it be that some of the ordinary star cities around us were once active galaxies or quasars? If so, are there still black holes in their cores?

In searching for more clues to the mysteries of the galaxies, our gaze turns to the universe as a whole. Then we discover another surprising fact about cities of stars.

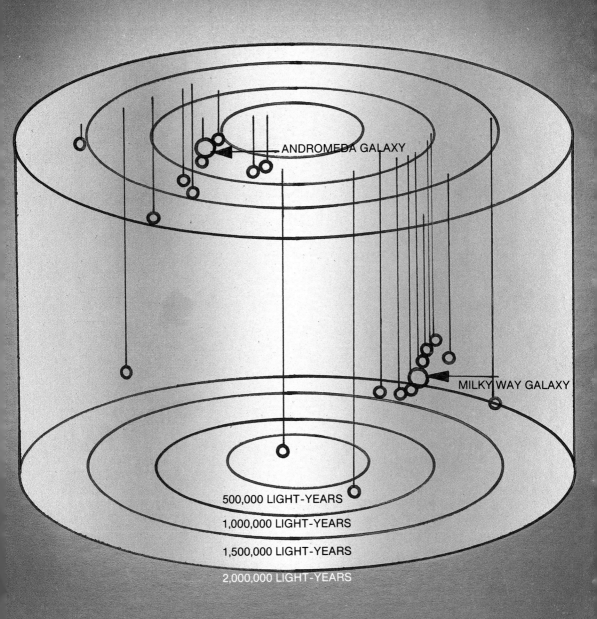

ANDROMEDA GALAXY

MILKY WAY GALAXY

500,000 LIGHT-YEARS

1,000,000 LIGHT-YEARS

1,500,000 LIGHT-YEARS

2,000,000 LIGHT-YEARS

ARRANGEMENT OF THE CLUSTER OF GALAXIES CALLED THE LOCAL GROUP

5 Clusters and Superclusters

Just as stars group together to form galaxies, so galaxies themselves group together to form **clusters of galaxies.** The Milky Way, for instance, is a member of a cluster of galaxies called the **Local Group.**

Our Galactic Neighborhood

Compared to other clusters, the Local Group, containing about 30 galaxies, is quite small. The Milky Way and another spiral star city, the **Andromeda Galaxy,** are its largest known members.

Most of the galaxies in the Local Group are irregulars or dwarf ellipticals. In fact, these seem to be the most common types of star cities throughout space.

Within a million light-years of the Milky Way there are ten small galaxies. The closest are the two Magellanic clouds, and beyond lies the much larger Andromeda spiral. At just over 2 million light-years from earth, the Andromeda Galaxy is the most distant object that we can see without a telescope.

All the members of the Local Group tug on each other through gravity. It is this force that holds the cluster loosely together. But if we go more than about 5 million light-years from home, we come to the edge of our galactic

47

neighborhood—and to the start of the far greater universe beyond.

Other Clusters of Galaxies

When we look outside the Local Group, we see many other clusters of galaxies. Some are small like our own. Others are very large, with hundreds or thousands of members.

Two of the most famous clusters are the Virgo Cluster, 65 million light-years away, and the Coma Cluster, 450 million light-years away. The Virgo Cluster contains more than a thousand galaxies, including the giant elliptical M87. The still larger Coma Cluster contains two giant ellipticals. In both cases, the gravity of the ellipticals is important in holding the clusters together.

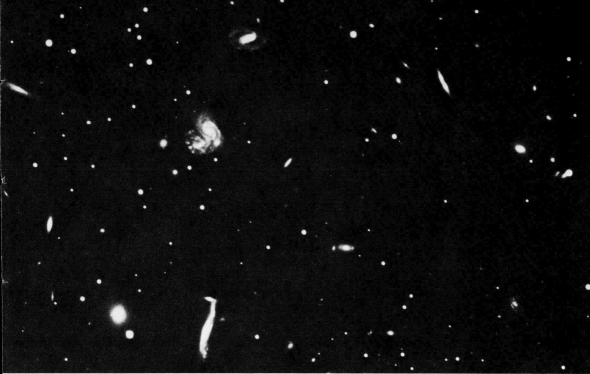

A cluster of galaxies in the constellation of Hercules is visible in this photo from the Kitt Peak National Observatory. The galaxies in this cluster are of various shapes and sizes.

Superclusters

In their studies of the universe, scientists have now discovered that there are **superclusters.** These are clusters of clusters of galaxies!

Our own Local Group is just one of hundreds of clusters that belong to the **Local Supercluster.** This huge group is centered on the Virgo Cluster—the biggest, heaviest cluster in our part of space. The Local Supercluster appears to be about 150 million light-years across.

As we look into the universe at large, we see other clusters and superclusters out to a distance of several billion light-years. Beyond that we see the quasars.

But the superclusters are not spread evenly over space. There are huge gaps—hundreds of millions of light-years across—where there are no galaxies at all. It

This galaxy in the constellation of Canes Venatici is many thousands of light-years across. But it is just one small part of a cluster of galaxies, and it is only a tiny part of a supercluster in the universe.

seems that the universe may be like an enormous sponge with great bubbles of empty space separating thin regions where there is matter.

Now we have reached the end of our galactic journey. In the future, we can look forward to many more exciting discoveries. The real adventure among the cities of stars has only just begun!

Appendix A:
Discover For Yourself

1. Explore the Galaxies

All the photographs of galaxies shown in this book were taken using giant telescopes. Although galaxies contain many stars, only a handful of them are bright and close enough to be seen with our eyes alone.

Closest of all is the Galaxy in which we live. Look up on a clear dark evening and you will see, scattered about, hundreds of stars. If there are no street lights close by, you may also see a faint, misty band stretching across the sky. This is the Milky Way—the thin disk of the Galaxy viewed edge-on. The best time to see the Milky Way is in September or October, when it passes directly overhead, going from northeast to southwest. Binoculars will show thousands of the distant stars that make up the Milky Way.

Also on view in the night sky from North America is our nearest large neighboring galaxy, the great spiral in

Andromeda. At a distance of just over 2 million light years, it is the farthest object we can see with our eyes alone. It looks like a very faint, fuzzy patch of light near the star Almaak (Gamma Andromedae) in Andromeda. You may need binoculars and a star map to help find it.

From southern countries, such as Australia, two other nearby galaxies can be seen. These are the large and small Magellanic clouds, a pair of irregular galaxies that are held by gravity to our own.

2. Make Star Counts

Begin by cutting out a square of stiff cardboard with sides six inches long. From the middle of this, then cut out a square hole with sides four inches long. You now have a frame with which to make star counts.

Take your frame, a pen, and paper, and choose a clear dark night as far away as possible from bright city lights. Hold the frame upright at arm's length.

First, pick a direction well away from the glowing band of the Milky Way. Hold the frame in this direction and count all of the stars you can see through it. Write this number down. Next, hold the frame in front of a part of the Milky Way. Take another count.

Repeat this several times, so that you have two columns of numbers: one of star counts in "dark" areas of the sky, the other of star counts in the direction of the Milky Way. What do you notice? What does this tell you about how stars, even those fairly close to the sun, are arranged in space? Compare your results with what you have already learned about the shape of our galaxy.

Appendix B:
Amateur Astronomy Groups
in the United States,
Canada, and Great Britain

For information or resource materials about the subjects covered in this book, contact your local astronomy group, science museum, or planetarium. You may also write to one of the national amateur astronomy groups listed below.

United States

The Astronomical League
Donald Archer,
   Executive Secretary
P.O. Box 12821
Tucson, Arizona 85732

American Association of
   Variable Star Astronomers
187 Concord Avenue
Cambridge, Massachusetts 02138

Great Britain

Junior Astronomical Society
58 Vaughan Gardens
Ilford
Essex IG1 3PD England

British Astronomical Assoc.
Burlington House
Piccadilly
London W1V 0NL England

Canada

The Royal Astronomical Society of Canada
La Société Royale d'Astronomie du Canada
Rosemary Freeman, Executive Secretary
136 Dupont Street
Toronto, Ontario M5R 1V2

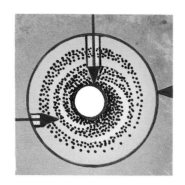

✸ Glossary

active galaxy—a type of galaxy that gives off much more energy than an ordinary galaxy

Andromeda Galaxy—the nearest large galaxy to our own. Like the Milky Way, it is a spiral

B-type star—a big, bright, hot kind of star. B-types are young stars that form in the arms of spiral galaxies

barred spiral—a type of spiral galaxy that has a bright bar running across its nucleus

billion—a thousand million. Written as 1,000,000,000

BL Lacertae object—a distant kind of galaxy whose nucleus looks very much like a quasar. BL Lacertae objects are also called "blazers" because they can blaze many times their normal brightness in just a short time

black hole—a region of or object in space whose gravity is so strong that nothing, not even light, can escape

cluster of galaxies—a group of galaxies, with a few dozen to more than a thousand members, that is bound together by gravity

core—the small region at the very center of a galaxy

corona—the huge region that has recently been discovered around our own and several other galaxies. It contains dark matter that makes up nine-tenths of the Galaxy's weight

disk—the flat, pancake-shaped part of a spiral galaxy in which the spiral arms lie

dwarf galaxy—an unusually small galaxy. "Dwarfs" are of two types—dwarf ellipticals and dwarf irregulars

elliptical galaxy—a type of galaxy, containing only old, red stars, that is round or oval in shape

energy—the ability to be active or do work. There are many forms of energy. Those made inside stars include radio waves, X rays, light, and heat

galactic—having to do with galaxies. The word comes from the ancient Greek *gala*, meaning milk

galactic cluster—a group of young stars, with a few hundred to a few thousand members, that is found in the disk of the Galaxy

galaxy—the largest grouping of stars in the universe. Galaxies are called "cities of stars"

giant galaxy—an unusually large galaxy. Largest of all are the giant ellipticals

globular cluster—a large, ball-shaped group of stars, with as many as a million members, bound together by gravity. Globular clusters contain old stars and are found in the halos of elliptical and spiral galaxies

gravity—the force by which all objects pull on all other objects. Gravity, for example, is what holds stars together in galaxies, and galaxies together in clusters of galaxies

halo—the large, round region of space around a spiral or elliptical galaxy that contains old stars and globular clusters

infrared—invisible energy waves that carry heat

irregular galaxy—a galaxy that, unlike spirals or ellipticals, has no definite shape

light-year—the distance traveled by light in one year. It is equal to about 6 trillion miles (9½ trillion kilometers)

Local Group—the small cluster of galaxies (about 30 in all) to which our own Milky Way belongs

Local Supercluster—the supercluster, measuring about 150 million light-years across, in which the Local Group is a member

Magellanic clouds—the two galaxies, both irregular, that are closest to our own

matter—anything that has weight and takes up space

Milky Way—the thin, ragged band of misty light that stretches across our sky from north to south. Made of distant stars, it is part of the disk of our galaxy seen edge-on

Milky Way Galaxy—the spiral galaxy in which we live

million—a thousand thousand. Written as 1,000,000

N-galaxy—a distant galaxy with a very bright, starlike nucleus that looks almost like a quasar

nucleus—the bright, bulging, middle part of a spiral galaxy that contains old, red stars

O-type star—the brightest, hottest kind of star. O-types are found in the gassy, dusty regions of spiral (and irregular) galaxies

Population I—the name given to the youngest objects within galaxies. Population I objects are only found in spirals and irregulars. They include O- and B- type stars, galactic clusters, and clouds of gas and dust

Population II—the name given to older objects within galaxies. They include the small, dim stars and globular clusters of the nuclei and halos

protogalaxy—a galaxy in the making. Protogalaxies probably formed from giant clouds of hydrogen gas in the early universe

quasars—the brightest, most distant objects known. Many scientists now think that quasars may be the very bright nuclei of young galaxies

radio galaxy—a galaxy, often appearing as a giant elliptical, that gives off an unusually large amount of radio waves
radio waves—weak, invisible waves of energy

satellite—an object that, because of gravity, orbits another (heavier) object
Seyfert galaxy—a rare kind of spiral galaxy that gives off huge amounts of energy from a small, starlike nucleus
solar system—the sun

plus all the objects that go around it, including: planets, moons, asteroids, meteors, and comets
spiral galaxy—a galaxy from whose center come bright, spiraling arms. The Galaxy we live in is a spiral galaxy
supercluster—a cluster of clusters of galaxies. Most galaxies belong to a cluster, and most clusters belong to a supercluster

trillion—a thousand billion. Written as 1,000,000,000,000

X rays—very powerful, invisible waves of energy. X rays are made only in special places, such as the atmospheres of stars

✳ Suggested Reading

Bok, Bart J. "A Bigger and Better Milky Way." *Astronomy,*
    January 1984, pp. 6-22.
Recently, it has been discovered that our galaxy is much
larger than we once thought. A famous astronomer explains
this new view of the Milky Way in an article filled with spec-
tacular pictures. (Advanced)

Bok, Bart and Priscilla. *The Milky Way.* Cambridge,
    Mass.: Harvard University Press, 1981.
A complete guide to the Galaxy in which we live by two of
the astronomers most involved in its discovery. (Advanced)

Ferris, Timothy. *Galaxies.* San Francisco: Sierra Club
    Books, 1980.
Today's large, modern telescopes have shown us still more of
the tremendous variety of star cities around us. Detail

within galaxies, never before seen, has now been made clear. This book contains dozens of galaxy pictures, together with an excellent accompanying text. (Intermediate-Advanced)

Kaufmann, William J. *Galaxies and Quasars.* New York: W.H. Freeman, 1979.
This book explores the makeup of galaxies and their possible link with quasars and other high-energy objects. (Advanced)

Marschall, Laurence A. "Superclusters: Giants of the Cosmos." *Astronomy,* April 1984, pp. 6-15.
A good, illustrated account of the latest findings on superclusters, the largest known structures in the universe. (Advanced)

Index